A IS FOR "ALL ABOARD!"

BY PAULA KLUTH & VICTORIA KLUTH
Illustrated by Brad Littlejohn

·P·A·U·L·H·
BROOKES
PUBLISHING CO ®

Baltimore • London • Sydney

Paul H. Brookes Publishing Co.
Post Office Box 10624
Baltimore, Maryland 21285-0624
USA

www.brookespublishing.com

Book design by Mindy Dunn.
Manufactured in China by JADE PRODUCTIONS.

Library of Congress Cataloging-in-Publication data
Kluth, Paula.
  A is for "all aboard" / by Paula Kluth and Victoria Kluth ; illustrated by Brad Littlejohn.
     p.   cm.
  ISBN-13: 978-1-59857-071-7 (hardcover)
  ISBN-10: 1-59857-071-4 (hardcover)
  1. Railroad trains—Juvenile literature.   I. Kluth, Victoria.   II. Littlejohn, Brad, ill.   III. Title.
  TF148.K56 2009
  625.1—dc22   2009020205

British Library Cataloguing in Publication data are available from the
British Library.

2013   2012   2011   2010   2009

10   9   8   7   6   5   4   3   2   1

To Dad & Dick

Our favorite trainmen on the

Green Bay & Western

When I was doing research for my book on literacy and autism, "*A Land We Can Share*": *Teaching Literacy to Students with Autism*, and learned the many ways alphabet books can profit literacy learners, I immediately began looking for ABC books on trains so that I could recommend and use them for my friends and students with autism. When I did not find a single train alphabet book for both young and older train enthusiasts, I asked my sister, Victoria, to help me write one.

As young children, my sister and I both loved trains and—because our father worked on the Green Bay & Western Railroad—spent a lot of time wandering around train yards, counting boxcars from the side of the road, and listening to stories from a brakeman's point of view. We wrote this book as a tribute to our dad and to his best friend and co-worker, Dick, and as a gift for our friends (including many on the autism spectrum) who love trains as much as we do! We hope you enjoy reading it as much as we enjoyed writing it.

Paula Kluth

IS FOR
"ALL ABOARD"

The conductor says, "All aboard"
to let passengers know that it is
time to get on the train.

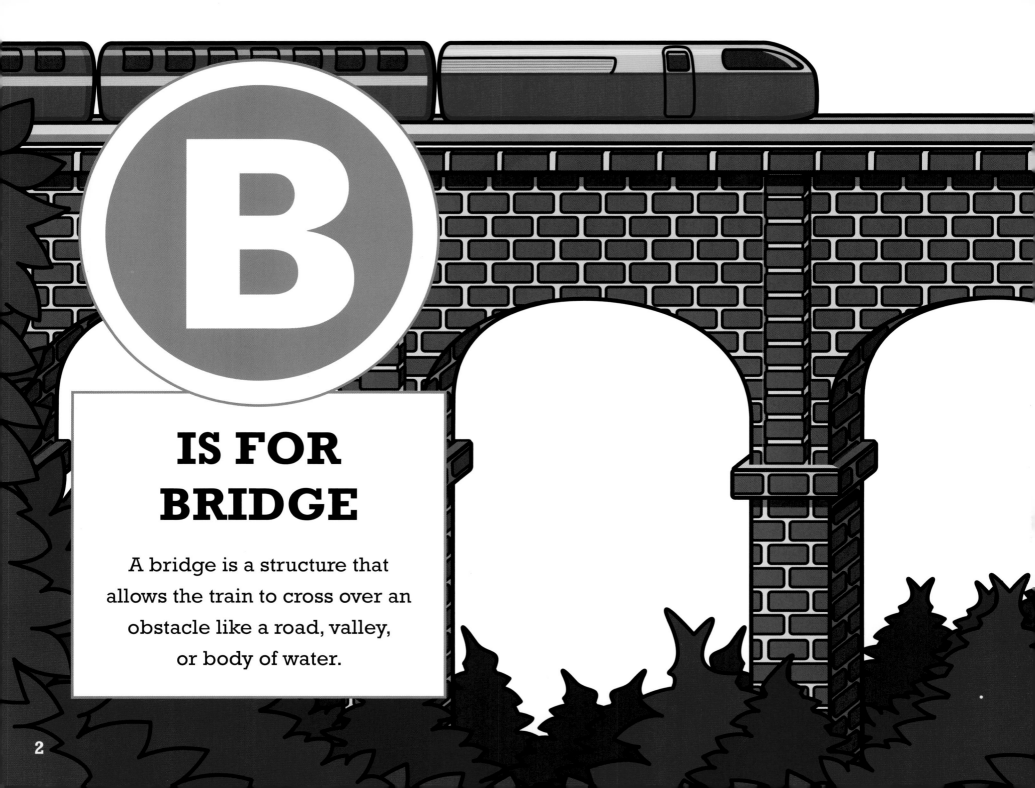

B

IS FOR BRIDGE

A bridge is a structure that allows the train to cross over an obstacle like a road, valley, or body of water.

C IS FOR CABOOSE

A caboose was a rail car used by the crew of the train, sometimes for sleeping. The caboose was usually the last car on the train.

D

IS FOR DOUBLE-DECKER

A double-decker is a train with two levels for passengers.

SOUTH STATION

E

IS FOR ENGINEER

The engineer is the person who operates the train.

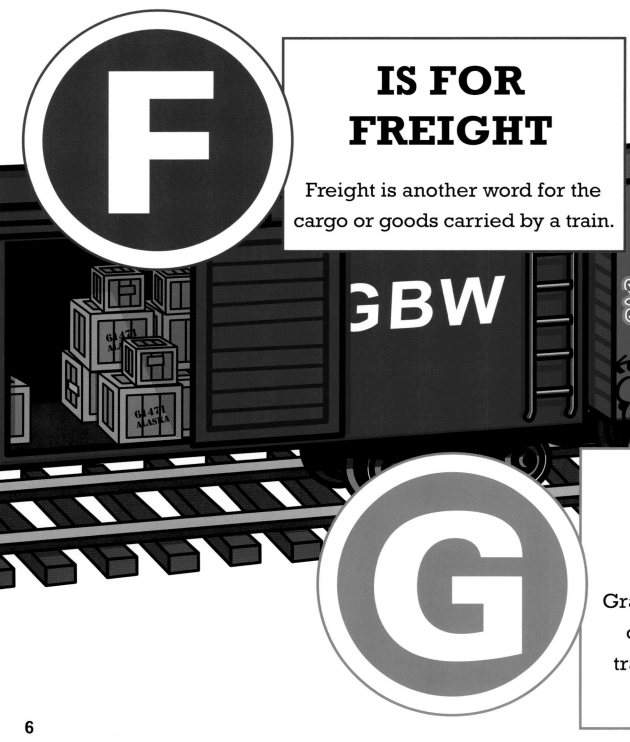

F

IS FOR FREIGHT

Freight is another word for the cargo or goods carried by a train.

G

IS FOR GRAFFITI

Graffiti is the name for words, symbols, or lettering that people paint on the train without getting permission from the railroad company.

6

H

IS FOR HEAD END

The front of the train is called the head end.

I

IS FOR IDLER CAR

An idler car carries no load
and creates an open space
between cars transporting freight
of unusual length,
such as pipe or poles.

J

IS FOR JIMMY

Jimmy is a nickname
for a coal car.

K

IS FOR KETTLE

A steam engine is sometimes called a kettle because of the cloud of steam that billows from it.

L

IS FOR LANTERN

Railroad workers used lanterns to signal instructions to one another. Lanterns were a way of communicating when the noise from the train made shouting or whistling too difficult.

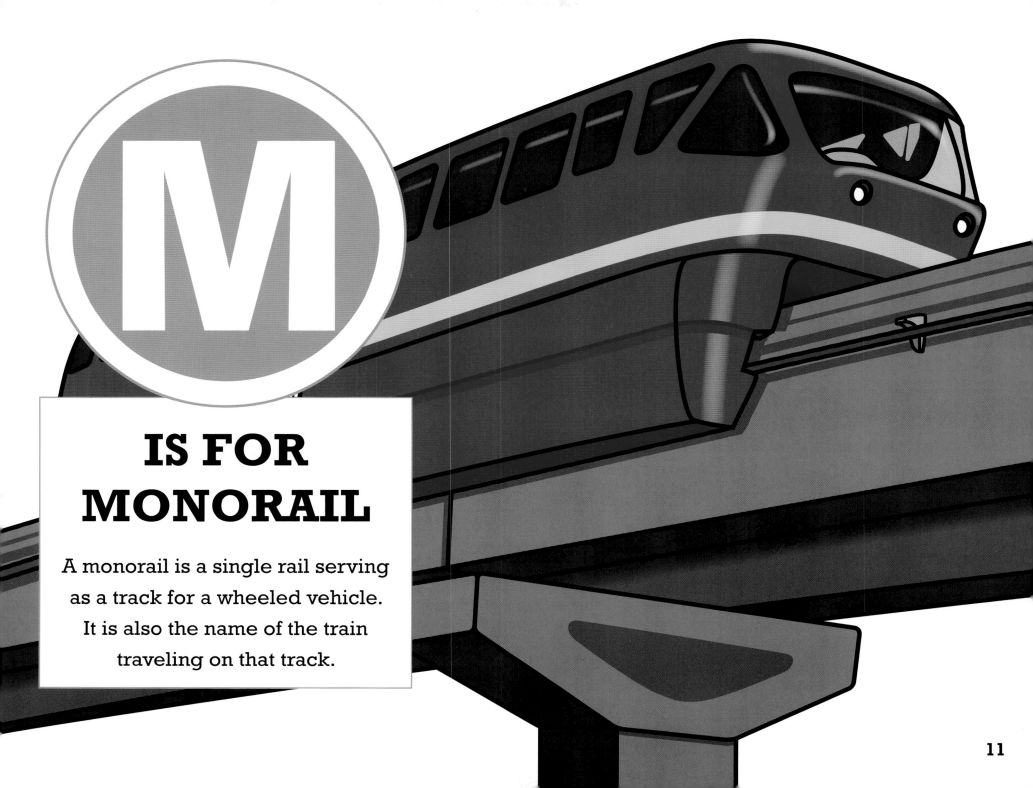

M

IS FOR MONORAIL

A monorail is a single rail serving as a track for a wheeled vehicle. It is also the name of the train traveling on that track.

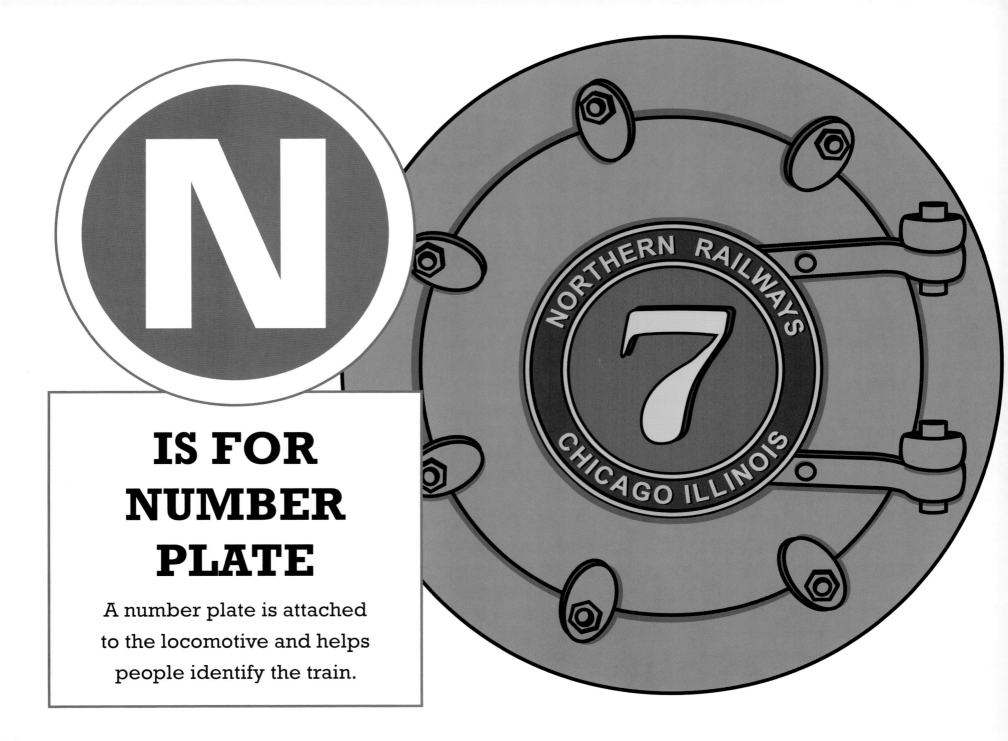

N

IS FOR NUMBER PLATE

A number plate is attached to the locomotive and helps people identify the train.

IS FOR ORIENT EXPRESS

The Orient Express is the name of a long-distance passenger train. The route has changed many times. Paris and Istanbul were its original endpoints.

France

Germany

Poland

Romania

Italy

Bulgaria

Paris

Istanbul

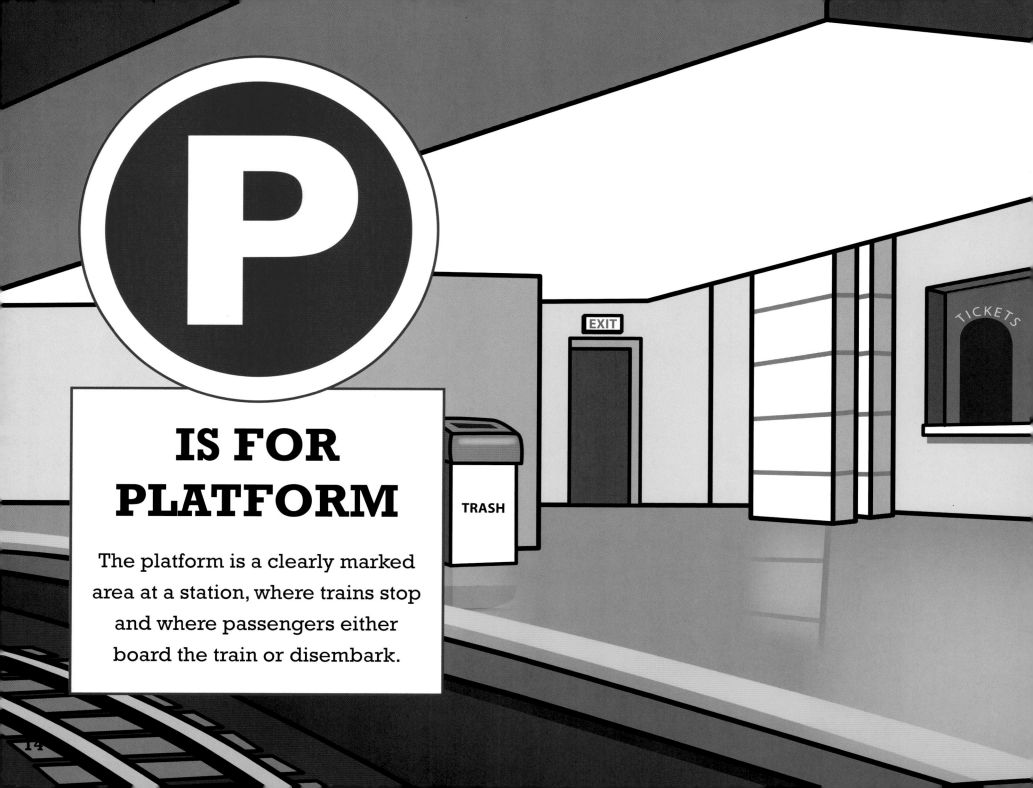

P

IS FOR PLATFORM

The platform is a clearly marked area at a station, where trains stop and where passengers either board the train or disembark.

Q

IS FOR
QUEUE

A queue is a line of people
waiting to get on the train.

R
IS FOR
RAIL TRACKS

Rail tracks, together with
railroad switches,
guide trains, making
steering unneccessary.

S
IS FOR
SIGNAL
TOWER

A signal tower is a building
from which railway points
and signals are controlled.

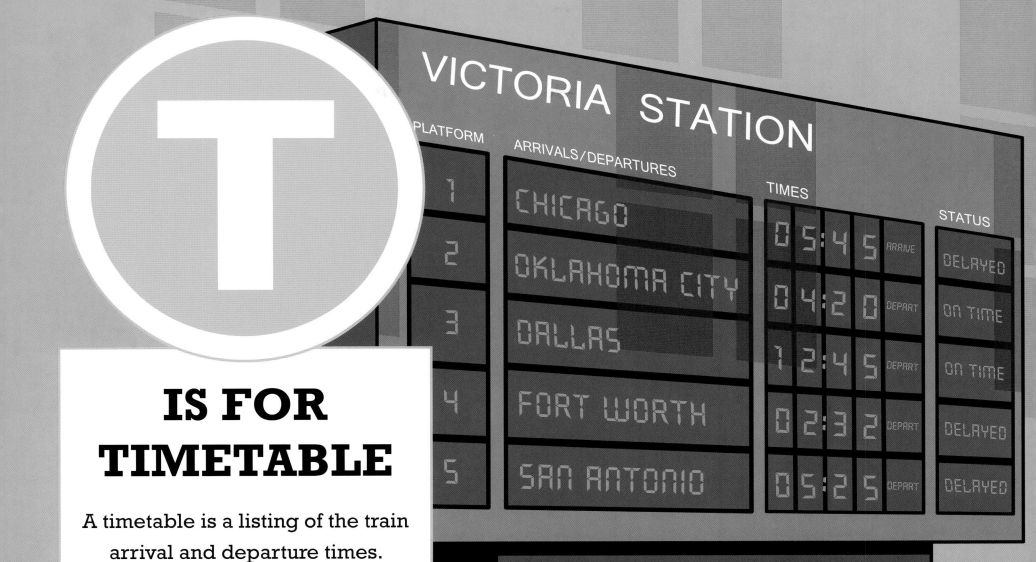

T

IS FOR TIMETABLE

A timetable is a listing of the train arrival and departure times.

IS FOR
UNIT TRAIN

A unit train's cars all start from
the same place and end at
the same destination.

V

IS FOR VARNISH

Varnish is a slang term used to refer to a passenger car or train.

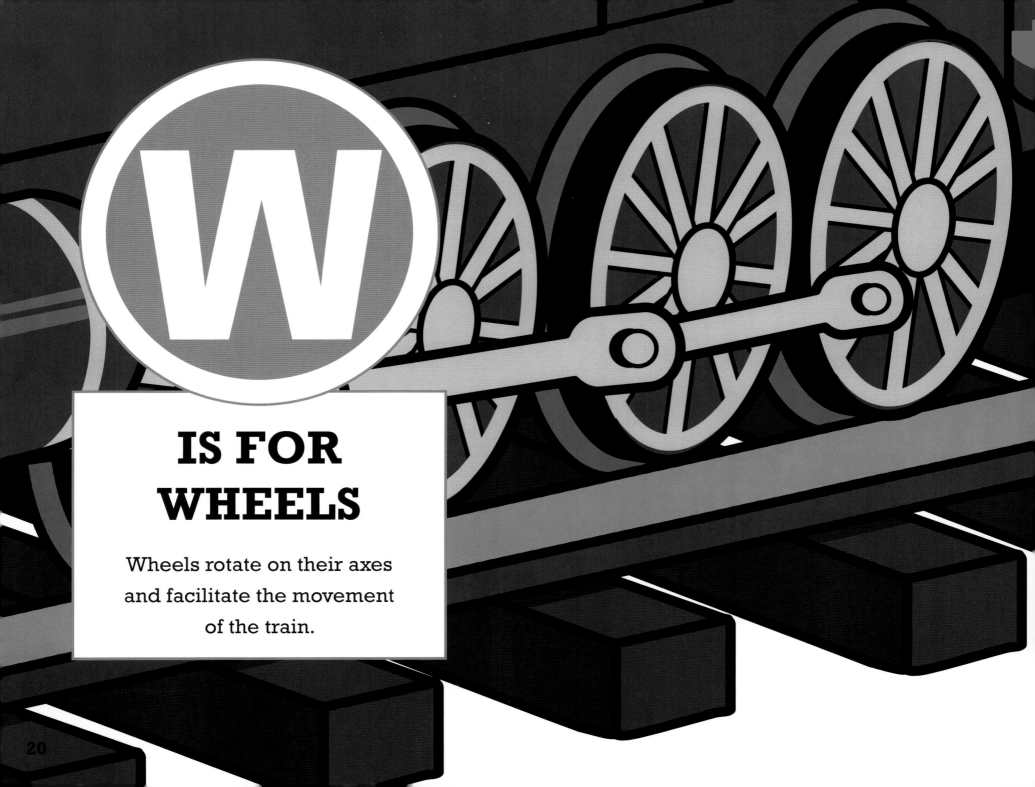

W

IS FOR WHEELS

Wheels rotate on their axes and facilitate the movement of the train.

IS FOR EXPRESS TRAIN

Instead of making every possible stop on a route, an express train picks up or drops off passengers at only a few stations. This way, it can get to its destination faster.

Y
IS FOR YARD

A yard is a system of tracks used to make up trains and store, sort, load, and unload cars.

WISCONSIN CENTRAL

Z

IS FOR ZEPHYR

The Zephyr was a speedy, diesel-powered train used in the mid-1900s to advertise passenger rail service. Its sleek design and shining, steel body earned it the nickname "Silver Streak."

USING ALPHABET BOOKS TO TEACH

Alphabet books meet a wide range of students' needs and interests. They not only provide emergent readers with opportunities for oral and written language development but also allow older students to experience a unique genre of books. Alphabet books can be used to introduce or provide an overview of a subject, to research a topic, or to get children interested in new vocabulary, art forms, or writing styles.

Many of you who are using this book may be interested in teaching a group of children, and others of you—especially parents—will be thinking only about how to reach one or just a few children. The tips we offer here should cover both of these audiences and give every parent, teacher, or child ideas for using this book in many different ways and for having fun with the words and pictures again and again.

- **Just enjoy.** Alphabet books, like picture books, are unique because children do not need to know the story or plot. For this reason, ABC books are great tools for encouraging independent exploration and sharing. Invite your child to "read" the book to you, even if she cannot decode the words or recall all of the terms.

- **Practice and learn.** As the child becomes familiar with the vocabulary and pictures in the book, ask him to go through and name everything he sees or remembers and tell you the names of the letters. Let him decide whether or not you should read the definitions.

- **Keep going.** On each page, parents and teachers can stop reading and ask the child to name other words that begin with the letter. Start with other train words and then move to other words in general.

- **Make it challenging.** Ask your child (or your students) to find other pictures on each page that represent the target letter (e.g., cupola on the caboose).

- **Encourage authorship.** After reading several different alphabet books, have the child create her own. After reading this book, the child may want to create her own railroad or train alphabet book or one on transportation in general. Or she may want to pick a completely different topic.

- **Investigate.** Ask the child to find out more about his favorite terms or illustrations. Look on the Internet for more photos of train bridges, or look through other books to research the Orient Express.

- **Read it again.** Having children read the same book repeatedly is a good way to improve reading fluency. Read *A Is for "All Aboard!"* several times with the child and then encourage her to read it to others.

- **Read as a team.** Read the book to the child. Then read again but, this time, have the child read right along with you as much as he can. This practice of reading in unison—called *choral reading*—is another great way to encourage and practice fluent reading.

- **Keep it fresh.** If your child enjoys reading this book over and over again, try to add something novel each time. On one occasion, point out the cover, the back cover, the title page, and the title. During another reading, ask the child to notice details in certain pictures or prompt her to predict or recall what she will find on the next page. All of this will help to build reading and writing skills.

- **Don't stop with this book.** Make many different alphabet books available to children so that they learn new vocabulary and content as well as letters and sounds.

Paula Kluth (on left), is one of today's most popular and respected experts on autism and inclusive education. Through her work as an independent consultant and the high-energy presentations she gives to professionals across the country, Dr. Kluth helps professionals and families create responsive, engaging schooling experiences for students with autism and their peers, too. An internationally renowned scholar and author, Dr. Kluth has written or co-written several books for Paul H. Brookes Publishing Co., including *"A Land We Can Share": Teaching Literacy to Students with Autism, "Just Give Him the Whale!": 20 Ways to Use Fascinations, Areas of Expertise, and Strengths to Support Students with Autism,* and *"You're Going to Love This Kid!": Teaching Students with Autism in the Inclusive Classroom.* Paula thinks trains are really neat and especially enjoys riding on "the EL" in Chicago.

Victoria Kluth (on right) lives in Melbourne, Australia, and works in sales. She loves trains and often rides on the Puffing Billy Railway in the Dandenong Ranges near her home. She also loves reading and enjoys sharing books with her two nieces. This is her first book for children.

Brad Littlejohn is a freelance illustrator and multimedia production artist from Denton, Texas. More samples of his art can be seen at bs-ink.com.